A Special Gift

for

Paul Knutson

**with congratulations
for graduating from**

Morgan Park Academy

Class of 1994

Presented by

Bob, Lisa, Hannah, Benjamin

We love you.

Letters from
the College Front

Letters from the College Front

Guys' Edition

Douglas P. Hutchcraft
Ronald P. Hutchcraft

BAKER BOOK HOUSE
Grand Rapids, Michigan 49516

Copyright © 1993 by Baker Books
a division of Baker Book House Company
P.O. Box 6287, Grand Rapids, MI 49516-6287

ISBN: 0-8010-4379-4

Third printing, January 1994

Printed in the United States of America

Produced by The Livingstone Corporation.
James C. Galvin and Daryl Lucas, project staff.

To the #2 man on my hero list.
Thanks for showing me Jesus, **Dad**.

Contents

Note to the Reader

They said, "You had to be there." This was all I heard when I asked people to explain what college life was like. That answer was unacceptable to me; there had to be some kind of map.

When I want directions to get somewhere, I usually ask someone who has been to that place already. That's why I sent all these letters to my brother Brad—so he could get an idea about school before he actually went. Usually it's not polite to read over someone's shoulder, but don't feel guilty about it. These letters are for you, too.

After each letter are some additional thoughts on the subject from my dad. We were all surprised he could remember good ideas from his days at Bedrock U., but maybe that's because he's been listening to and helping guys like us for thirty years.

This new territory of college can be exciting—if you've got a good map. Thanks for picking up this book. I sincerely hope and pray it will be a little help in facing what will turn out to be a big challenge . . . and a lot of fun.

Thanks,

It's Here!

Dear Brad,

It's here, and it's here in full force. I can't believe my first week of college is behind me; I can't believe that I'm here in the first place!

What happened? It doesn't seem too long ago I was carrying my "CHiPs" lunch box to kindergarten. (Don't tell anyone I used it in high school too, OK Brad?) And was it fourteen years ago I got over my crush on Ms. Feefinshneitzer? Unbelievable.

Elementary school went by quickly, but nothing breezed by as quickly as high school. I can still hear the ringing in my ears from my teachers and guidance counselors chanting, "S . . . A . . . T! . . . S . . . A . . . T!" In fact, the time between looking foolish for not knowing where my locker was as a freshman and looking foolish for wearing a "distinguished" graduation gown as a senior just flew by. Man, what happened to high school?

I know what happened. The future got here, and it got here fast. All the preparation, the anxiety, the coloring in the lines . . . it all comes down to this: college.

As if I weren't feeling old enough as it is, Mom and Dad just called and reminded me that you will be graduating this year. Let me tell you, there are already some things I wish I had learned before I got here. I tell you what, maybe I'll write to you once in a while and fill you in on things I'm learning as

I go along. Hopefully it'll make things a little easier on you when you get here.

I know, I know. Just call me "Mother Doug." But I wish someone had done it for me, so I'm gonna do it for you.

Happy studying!

Your bro,

Doug

A Word about Beginning College

Perms aren't.

Sure, the hair stylist says all that kinky hair is a perm. But ask how long the curls will last. "Oh, two or three months." Now wait a minute—that's not a perm . . . that's a temp!

Today you stand on top of a mountain that took you twelve years (or longer?) to climb—Mt. Senior. And from that vantage point, you can see what most people in high school miss . . . the difference between what's "temp" and what's "perm."

The big party, the big game, the big crush—they all look very temporary as you look back from Mt. Senior. The perms? They are the lives of people for whom you made a difference.

I think there ought to be a "Make a Difference" yearbook. It wouldn't be like the classic yearbook, with your smiling picture and a list of your activities. "Soccer 1, 2; Chess Club 4; Nintendo 3, 4; Central Detention 1, 2, 3, 4." No—those are temps. Instead this yearbook would show your picture and next to it a list of the people who would say, "You made the difference for me." That's permanent.

You don't have much time left before you say good-bye to all your high school friends—many of whom you'll never see again, unless you take them to heaven with you. In these closing days on Mt. Senior, be sure you have told your friends about Jesus and how they can know him. They may or may not listen. They may file the information away and come back to Jesus later in life. But you won't have to live with the regrets of letting them go without letting them know.

Mt. Senior actually gives you a view in two directions— not just looking back at high school, but looking ahead at that next exciting mountain. Ahead of you is Mt. College and one of life's priceless moments . . . a NEW BEGINNING.

Leave your high school masks in high school. Decide the "you" that you want to be before Day One of college ever hits. Take an honest look at the weaknesses and bad habits that tended to trip you up over the past four years and get them under control now.

In fact, the months or weeks between Mt. Senior and Mt. College are a time to get your life under control. There will be plenty of craziness to handle in college. Take these "in between" days to get you together.

And no matter how you decide to wear your hair, concentrate on the perms.

College Food
and College Fat

Dear Brad,

Boy, I've been in college for only a short time, and I've already gained something I didn't come here with. Four pounds and love-handles. Yes, here at college I've been introduced to the wonderful concept of unlimited food!

I've never seen so much food in my whole life. Each day the cafeteria offers new chances to choose, new chances to socialize, and new chances to eat like a starved pig. It doesn't help that the people who prepare our food seem to be oblivious to the countless cholesterol, fat, and diet precautions our country has so graciously provided.

Before I arrived I heard horror stories about the "freshman fifteen." (This phrase refers to the poundage put on during your initial year at college.) Fifteen is bad enough, but at the rate I'm going I'll gain the "freshman fifty."

It isn't just the meals that get me into trouble. When you start studying until three in the morning, you find yourself getting hungry and searching for anything that will keep you awake. That "something" is usually a pepperoni pizza.

There are some things you can do to counter some of the caloric land mines you'll face. The smartest and easiest idea is to get in shape before you get to college. This gives you some pounds to work with.

Once you're here, if you follow some guidelines for yourself, you'll stay out of trouble. On nights when you know you'll be up late studying, make sure you eat light during the day. And when you do snack late, try to keep it to fruit, popcorn, or possibly tree bark. (Just kidding!)

Finally, if you have a metabolism like mine (sloooww), the most important rule to stick by is a regular exercise program. Time is limited, but if you incorporate exercise into your schedule before classes start and keep it a priority, you shouldn't have too much trouble fitting it in.

Well, I've got to go and order my pizz . . . er, fruit basket now. I'll write again later!

Your bro,
"Jack LaLanne"

A Word about Food

"And . . . in this corner . . . weighing in at 210 pounds . . . Round Ron Hutchcraft!"

That's how they could have introduced me my first day at college. At only five feet eight inches tall, I was the original blimp.

And it didn't feel very good. I entered my "new beginning" feeling self-conscious about my weight. I was anxious to meet all those new girls, but not sure they would want to meet me.

I learned a lesson late that I hope you learn early—enter college in the best physical shape you can. Get your body under control before you enter Appetite City.

Appetites often rule people in college. It was meant to be the other way around. You will self-destruct if you don't control the college appetites that scream, "Feed me! Sex me! Sedate me!" In the Bible, the apostle Paul says the one who "gets the prize" is the one who "goes into strict training." Paul even went so far as to say, "I beat my body and make it my slave" (1 Cor. 9:24–27).

So learn to say no to that body of yours. If your body is under control when college comes, you'll be ready for the social opportunities . . . and ready for an intense load of responsibilities.

If you're carrying an intense load of Twinkies and Big Macs around your middle, dump it now. Don't eat after 5:30 at night, weigh yourself regularly, exercise at night, go to bed hungry, anticipate "pig" times by losing so you can gain without damage. And once you get your weight off, set a weight boundary and never cross it. When you get to it, reverse all engines!

If your appetites, your hormones, and your glands run you, you'll be a slave all through college. So make sure your body knows who's boss before you take it to Appetite City.

Take It or Leave It

Dear Brad,

I can't believe how hot it is here. I thought September was supposed to be a relief! Dear brother, I sweat as I write, but write I will.

Do you remember when I was about thirteen and you were eleven? If you remember, neither of us had reached our full muscular potential, and yet we were forced . . . er, asked, to carry out the worst sentence parents can inflict on their young sons; we were driven along to carry Lisa's luggage. From that day on, any time our wonderful sister had any luggage to bring anywhere, we were expected to do the honors of carrying it. This sentence probably would not have been so bad if Lisa hadn't insisted on carrying her whole wardrobe everywhere she went. Anyway, I'm not really complaining . . . Mom and Dad did pay for the hernia operation.

Things were bad up to that point, but nothing could have prepared us for Black Thursday . . . the day Lisa left for college. Suitcase after suitcase, bag after bag . . . oh, the horror. That was six years ago. I recovered last week. You know, I never understood why she brought all that stuff . . . until I got here. And, dear brother, this is why I'm writing you today. There's stuff you just don't need to bring to college . . . and stuff you dare not forget.

So, what to bring? Well, you know the obvious stuff (I think) like underwear, socks, etc. But there's some stuff I didn't think of before I got to college that I wished I had once I got here. For example, it would have been nice if I had remembered to bring quarters to feed the laundry machines. Stamps are good, too; you'll find they'll save you thousands of dollars in phone bills. And if you value having any knowledge about the world outside of your dorm room, it's good to have a magazine subscription to something other than *Sports Illustrated*. It's wise to bring a general knowledge of computers with you; you'll find they are an integral part of many of your classes. (Don't freak out. Just know how to turn the thing on and off, and work from there.)

What else? Here's a general list of stuff you might want to think about: anything you want to decorate your room with, clothes for all kinds of weather, your pillow, personal items you use to make yourself presentable in the morning, an iron, a power strip (the dorm room doesn't come with unlimited outlets), an extra pair of glasses (these are usually needed only when you wear them in the first place), and, perhaps the most important thing, a computer or word processor.

For everything you forget to bring, there is something you bring that you don't need. For example, it's not vital that you bring your whole wardrobe; just bring the clothes you know you'll wear. And you might as well forget any excess books; you'll have plenty of reading to occupy you once you get here.

To be honest, Brad, there's no way I can cover everything in one letter because each person is different. I guess the best way to pack for college is to mentally go through a normal day and bring everything you'll need. I know there will be some stuff you overlook, and you'll bring some stuff you wish you hadn't. But hopefully this letter can be of use to you. As that old saying goes, "An ounce of prevention is worth bringing too many clothes."

Your bro,

[signature: Doug]

A Word about Stuff

Rabbits and stuff. They both multiply fast.

You've had eighteen years to accumulate your own personal mountain of stuff—clothes you'll never wear again except on Nerd Day, old toys, books, papers, fossilized pizza crusts.

Now it's time to do yourself a favor . . . un-stuff your life! This countdown to college offers you a natural break in your life, a time to get things under control before the college-quake hits.

This is your golden opportunity to simplify your life. So clobber those closets, dive into those drawers, plunder those piles, battle those bags.

Sell what you can to help with those college bills.

Better yet, "Give to the poor" (Luke 12:33). Some of our warmest family memories are of scouring the house for stuff—good stuff—so we could take it to some homeless people. Why should we have three or six of something when others don't even have one of it?

With your life "un-stuffed," you can leave behind a home base that's sane and simplified.

It's a great feeling knowing you have what you need—and that's all. You've got an exciting marathon ahead of you. When you travel light, you can run well.

Being Your Own Mother

Dear Brad,

It was dark . . . oh, so dark. I silently tiptoed through the wreckage, trying desperately to reach my final destination. The terrain was grueling; the stench, unbearable. But I had to press on. Then, I felt it. A horrible something, grabbing, reaching for my legs. It had me! It had me! I wrestled and fought to no avail. I couldn't get loose! This . . . this blob would not let me go! Fighting for breath and my own survival as I fell to my knees, I heard a voice—a familiar one—call to me the only instructions that would save me from this terrible foe!

"Doug, why don't you just do your laundry?"

"I don't have any idea how to!" The darks, the whites, the faded, and the brights! . . . What's a man to do?

Brad, I'm sorry I had to recount this horror story to you, but it's for your own good. This is a (somewhat) true story of my first encounter with my own laundry. This first encounter happened right here at college, and it was a terrifying experience. But laundry is just one of the reasons I am writing to you today. There are many things I was forced to learn once I got to college.

College is a time where you learn to be your own mother. All those "small" things Mom does for you while you live at home turn into "big" things once you hit campus. There are a select few whose mothers foresaw this problem and who already know how to do "motherly" things. However, this letter is for you, Brad, a man who I know has little experience in the field of mothering.

You know, I never realized how silly one can look wearing a shirt that looks like Sammy Davis, Jr., tap-danced on it. Yes, one of the joys I had to learn here at the big "C" was ironing. I tend to be one of those who learns his craft by the trial-and-error process, as many of my shirts with dark brown triangles on them will demonstrate.

Laundry is a big problem as well. I suggest you learn at least the fundamentals of this craft before you get to college, or you may find yourself wearing a lot of multicolored underwear.

Oh, and yes, I've saved the best craft for last. Have you ever noticed how the bathroom at home stays spotlessly clean? Guess what? To my surprise, it didn't stay that way because it cleaned itself. Mom did it! And because Mom doesn't live here with me, I have to clean the bathroom myself. You can just leave your bathroom alone if you want to, but you'll have to get used to the shrubbery that begins to grow around the shower and the biology majors who come to study the organisms in your toilet.

Brad, I could go on and on about stuff I had to learn here, but I wouldn't want to bore you or, worse yet, gross you out. I will say that it's an extremely wise idea to learn this stuff before you make that trek to your learning institution.

It can get awfully expensive to fly your mother out to school every weekend.

Your bro,
Mr. Mom

A Word about Being Your Own Mother

"We didn't pay any attention."

That's how the soldier described the reaction to classes on chemical warfare during boot camp. But the interview with him was taking place on the border of Saudi Arabia and Kuwait on the eve of the Persian Gulf War. Things had changed. *"They're teaching us about chemical warfare again. Man, are we paying attention now!"* Of course! With Saddam Hussein's chemical weapons just over the border, they knew they would need that information.

For you, the freedom and responsibility of college life are just over the border. Yea! And, uh-oh! There are lots of everyday skills you haven't paid much attention to before, but now you need to know them. You're almost on your own!

So eliminate a lot of college stress . . . and be sure you can answer yes to questions like these before you kiss Mom or Dad good-bye:

- *Do I know how to make and live on a budget?*
- *Can I manage a checkbook?*
- *Do I know how to do laundry? Ironing?*
- *Do I know about oil changes, tune-ups, changing a tire, and all the other things it takes to keep a car running?*
- *Do I know how to save money on phone calls by calling at cheaper times of the day and not using the expensive operator-assisted calls?*
- *Do I know Mom's grocery-store savings tricks?*

Maybe you've never paid much attention to life's basic survival skills before. Pay attention now. There's little time to learn them once the battle begins.

To Drive or Not to Drive

Dear Brad,

God is awesome. A "special friend" and myself just took a drive and caught some of the beautiful foliage that comes to these parts this time of year. I'd like to tell you more, but I think I'll "leaf" it alone for now.

How's my favorite brother doing? I'm doing great, and I'm actually not too busy unless you consider five papers and three tests within the next two days a lot of work. How's your "special friend"? Did you have to sell any relatives yet to pay for your dates? If so, write me and tell me which ones so I can revise my Christmas shopping list.

Well, enough small talk. I'm writing to inform you of an interesting problem just about every freshman runs into. It's called "Wow, I'm bored. I wish I had a car" syndrome. I don't think that's official medical terminology, but it's close enough. As you probably know, a lot of colleges, especially smaller, private ones, won't allow freshmen to have a car on campus unless they have an extraordinary reason, like a work commute to Anchorage or something. If you end up going to a larger state school, they'll allow you to have a car, but you will probably end up having some of the same problems that someone at a smaller school has.

I suppose it's around Thanksgiving that freshmen who don't have a car on campus start getting enough confidence to lift up their heads, look around, and realize that it could get pretty boring around campus without any wheels. Then it's right after

Thanksgiving break that upperclassmen with a car have to start hiding their keys and themselves from what I like to affectionately call the "car monsters."

Car monsters are freshmen who, no matter the cost or inconvenience, are convinced that they must have a car for the weekend or they will die. Brad, this is a dangerous species, and you should avoid getting messed up with them at all costs. Beside the fact that these students think they are better than all the other freshmen stuck on campus, they also are taking irresponsible risks for themselves and the car owners. Guess what? For some reason, insurance companies don't take kindly to other drivers cracking up your car. In other words, if one of the "car monsters" crashes your car, your insurance will go up about $50,000. Well, that's an exaggeration, but it might as well be that much.

In return for cracking up the car, the freshman who was irresponsible enough to use it will be indebted to the car owner. In case you haven't gotten the point yet, I'm saying wait until you have your own car.

On the other hand, at bigger universities, some freshmen are "lucky" enough to have a car. Just so you know, I'll let you in on a couple secrets about this. First of all, because you're a freshman, you get last parking choices. This means you could very well end up parking in a small town in Montana. The other problem is for any student who has a car—automotive maintenance. For some reason, before I got to college no one informed me of the joys of taking care of a car. First of all, it's big money. By the time you have to pay for your own gas, own car repairs, own car washes, own oil changes, etc., etc., you could spend your whole family's inheritance.

Having a car on campus can turn into a big hassle. When others who don't have a car find out you do, you'll either end up starting your own taxi service or you'll have to go through the trouble of turning down a lot of puppy-dog eyes.

Well, I've got to sign off, but before I go I want to say that having a car at college can be a good thing, as long as you are responsible and realistic about it. It's not all fun and games, and there are a lot of hidden costs and hassles that you should take into consideration before you bring the ol' Ford to campus. But as for you, Brad, it doesn't look like you're going to have a choice. So, "happy walking!"

Your brother turned mechanic,

Doug

A Word about Transportation

Poor Gilligan. He and his friends were trapped on that island for years.

That "trapped on an island" feeling sometimes hits you in college. And a car is your S. S. Minnow with which to escape.

But whenever you're looking at the car option, don't just look at the pluses . . . there's a price tag, too. Here are three mistakes to avoid:

1. *Underestimating the cost. Cars have to be fed, bathed, fixed. They can make an already tight college budget melt down.*

2. *Underestimating the line at your door.* Just when you're trying to figure out how to manage your time, the "I need a ride" line forms outside your room. It's nice to be needed, but this much?
3. *Underestimating the temptation.* Studies have shown that students with cars generally don't do as well academically. Frankly, a car can be a "Fatal Distraction" and a temptation few can handle. It's just too tempting to say "yes" to your wheels and "later" to your homework. If you do have a car, use it as a reward, not an escape. Don't play until you've finished your work.

Focus—that's what College: Year One will require. You need to stay on the island and master living there. Be careful of having a car to escape in. . . . That car could end up sinking you.

Secular or Christian?

Dear Brad,

What's up? How are things at home? (I heard Dad and the dog aren't getting along too well.) I'm glad you wrote to me and expressed your concern for your friends. You're right—it is difficult for them to decide whether they should go to a secular or a Christian college. I just thought I'd write today and maybe help clear some things up for you guys.

There are some definite advantages and disadvantages of going to either kind of school. At a secular school, a Christian has many more chances to spread the gospel.

Another advantage is the definite challenge your faith will encounter. A secular college is full of students and teachers who couldn't care less about the God you serve. Patiently enduring this kind of adversity could be a great faith sharpener.

An important thing you've got to keep in mind is this: You can't make a school decision based on these factors until you have honestly evaluated the strength of your faith. Are you capable at this point of standing up to all this? If you aren't (and many aren't yet), you endanger yourself with the possibility of getting sucked into the sin that will surround you.

What about Christian schools? Believe it or not, Christian colleges can confront you with the same challenges as secular colleges. Christian campuses, though definitely filled with people who serve God, aren't as "spiritual" as you might think. Your faith, though not always directly challenged, is tested in other ways. It's very easy to get in a Christian "rut." It may be as hard to stay out of this rut as it is to have your faith persecuted. Because I've attended both secular high school and Christian college, I can attest to that.

But a Christian college can also be a great place to have your faith sharpened. I have found it's just as hard (if not harder) to challenge stagnant Christians as it is to challenge stubborn non-Christians.

So what to do? Both kinds of colleges have their good and bad points, but I lean toward the Christian college experience. You can sharpen your faith at either kind of college, and you can be a good influence at either on those who don't care as much about the Lord as you do. But there are two reasons why I think a Christian college is a better idea.

The biggie is this: education. You'll learn the same math and history at both colleges, but only the Christian college will offer the Christian perspective. Only the Christian college will offer the kind of Bible courses that agree with and strengthen what you believe.

You'll have the rest of your life to face the secular world in the workplace. I look at college as a time to interact with the Christian community and "fuel up," spiritually and academically, for those years ahead.

Well, I've gotta run. Hang in there.

Your bro,

A Word about Choosing Between Secular and Christian Colleges

I'll bet you didn't know you were so popular. When you became a senior, your mailbox started to explode with college mail. You have probably been contacted by everyone from Aristotle Engineering to Zephaniah Bible College. Isn't it great to be in such demand—and so confused?

In this blizzard of possibilities, you have to sort out one of the most life-shaping choices you'll ever make: "Shall I go to a secular or a Christian college?"

No matter which you choose, you'll have opportunities to enjoy and dangers to avoid. At a secular school, you won't go to the party as people did in high school—you'll live at the party. A Christian college won't be like going to church so much as living at the church.

If you live at the "party," you can go to pieces spiritually. If you live at the "church," you can go to sleep.

You're not just choosing a place to study a major . . . you're choosing your environment and relationships for the next four years. Yes, it is an important decision—one that you and God need to work on together. As you weigh your options, keep the following questions in mind.

If you're considering a secular school, ask yourself:

1. Will I choose Jesus' uniform from Day One at college? You cannot "serve two masters" (Matt. 6:24)—wear the jersey of one team and the helmet of the other. You'll never make it if you don't go publicly, totally Christian right from the kickoff.

2. Am I a "debriefing" person? You will be bombarded every day with godless ideas and life-styles, and you'll need to be the kind of person who talks through it with another believer. Otherwise, you will just soak up the lies until they erode your faith.
3. Did I stand consistently against the dark pressures in high school? If you didn't stand by Jesus in the part-time darkness of high school, how will you stand in the full-time darkness of a secular college?
4. Will I immediately connect with God's family at my school? God has His kids everywhere—your first mission is to find the Christians and Christian groups at your school. Following Christ is a family affair, not a Lone Ranger experience. At a secular college, more than most any other place, "let us not give up meeting together, . . . but let us encourage one another" (Heb. 10:25).

God is looking for some dedicated disciples to make a powerful difference for Him in a secular college—maybe He's sending you. If Jesus assigns you to be His lifeguard there, just be sure you're strong enough to avoid getting dragged under.

Now if you're considering a Christian school, ask yourself:

1. Am I more concerned with what pleases Jesus than with what most Christians are doing? Because the sacred gets so familiar, a lot of students get cynical about what God calls holy, or they get care-

less or rebellious or hard. If you tend to look to Christians more than Christ, you'll probably catch terminal sleeping sickness.

2. Do I tend to get close to Christian friends who are serious about Jesus? A Christian college is not heaven, or even close. The people who go there come in the same flavors as those in your youth group. So under the word *Christian* will be everything from spiritual radicals to spiritual rebels. Your choice of friends will make the difference between a Christian coma or a Christian conquest. "He who walks with the wise grows wise, but a companion of fools suffers harm" (Prov. 13:20).

3. Will I find a personal mission off campus? Disadvantaged kids to tutor . . . evangelizing teenagers . . . lonely senior citizens . . . an outreach coffee house—it's exercise that will keep all that Bible-banquet from turning to fat. A mission will keep you awake and sharp.

As you make your college choice, remember that you have three basic assignments from God for these next four years:

1. To develop your God-given gifts "to the max."
2. To make a Jesus-difference in the place God sends you.
3. To establish the network of relationships and views on which you will build the rest of your life.

31

You need to ask your Lord, "Where can I do that best?" Offer him a blank piece of paper to write His plans on. "Trust in the LORD with all your heart and lean not on your own understanding; in all your ways acknowledge Him, and He will make your paths straight" (Prov. 3:5-6).

Secular or Christian? Ironically, the bottom line is the same both places: Does your Christianity consist of you and your environment . . . or you and Jesus?

Extracurricular Buffet

Dear Brad,

> *Gonna tell a little story 'bout a man named Steve*
> *Signed up for every club his eyes did see*
> *Signed up for even more*
> *Studies went out the door*
> *And now his G.P.A. stinks.*

Hey, I never said I was a poet. Anyway, this is the true story of many college freshmen. The "extracurricular buffet" is, like any dinner buffet, fun to choose from. But take in too much and you'll feel bloated. Brad, I'm writing today to give you a few ideas on how to handle the bevy of extracurricular activities you'll be free to choose from once you hit the college trail.

There's an interesting phenomena at college: Even though there is much less free time than high school, there are many more activities to choose from. This can get kind of frustrating, especially if there are many activities you're interested in joining.

The best way to make decisions on how much to join is to keep the right perspective on your time at college. Your number one job here is to study. Everything else comes second. If you don't believe me, try to see how many employers will give you a job based on your activity in the chess club.

As far as what to join, that's up to you. You can be confident that there will be something you'll want to join. Most colleges offer everything from swimming to Swahili lessons.

Just keep in mind that once you've joined, you've made a commitment to that particular group. So you need to be sure that the activity is really worth all the time you will invest in the months ahead.

My final advice on this topic is: No matter how tempting all the offers may be, in your first semester join only one thing and see how the time you spend with that corresponds with your study time. You'll have plenty of time after that to work from there.

I've gotta get going—the Armpit Noises Club has a competition tonight.

Your bro,

Doug

A Word about the Extracurricular Buffet

extra \ 'ek-stre \ adj.: beyond what is usual or necessary

If all that senior year mail from 628 colleges made you feel wanted, wait until orientation week at college. You'll be pursued by choirs, clubs, publications, organizations—the "Body Snatchers" trying to sign you up for their "extra."

You may be tempted to sign up for six or seven of them. Don't. Learning to manage major-league studying and your own life will take more of you than you think.

So keep the main thing the main thing—your studies! A lot of college freshmen make a major mistake—over-commitment. If you add more than one or two "extras," you may meet the ugliest "pro" on campus . . . pro-bation. That's the academic "do or die" pressure you feel all through second semester because your grade point didn't make it first semester.

Now it isn't that you should live in the library for four years. Just be selective in choosing an extracurricular activity—one from which you can profit and grow the most. Then, as your college career goes on, you can add or substitute other activities. It's not good to be Joe One-Dimension. The right balance helps you become a well-rounded person (so does college food!).

And don't get so tied up in on-campus extras that you don't have time for an off-campus mission for Jesus. Balance also means getting out of the college cocoon and carrying the light to the world.

You have a great four-year race ahead of you . . . and a good run depends on a good start. Don't try to carry too much with you on your first lap.

Hitting the Books

Dear Brad,

In my last couple of letters I kind of skipped over the subject of studying. But to get to studying, you have to fight an ugly monster who's devastatingly hard to conquer, yet must be challenged each and every day. I lovingly call this monster the "Time Consumer."

You know how easy it was in high school. Because I was fairly bright, I seldom had to study very hard, much less pay attention in class. The class I worked the hardest in was Foods 1, and that was only because I wanted to eat pancakes every day.

Then I got to college. Do you remember Harold Fitzwater? You remember, the pizza delivery guy? He told me college wasn't much different. He told me it would be a party. What Harold Fitzwater didn't tell me was that he flunked out of community college with a −1.4 G.P.A.

So, there's no more getting away with not studying. It's as simple as this ancient proverb:

There was a young man who played the fool
Though his brain was very bright.
He didn't study in high school—
Now his grades are lower than a snake's belly.

Ah, now that's poetry. Anyway, you've got to come into college with good study habits, or your grades will suffer a slow death.

So how do you avoid the freshman grade slump? I've picked up a couple of good ideas from upperclassmen.

First of all, there is no longer a designated "study time." Studies are a full-time job. You can't wake up in the morning and expect to party all day with your friends. When you wake up, say, "Today is a work day." If free time comes along (it usually will), then great. But learning is first priority.

Brad, I'm going to say one word. Here let me whisper it . . . come closer . . . closer . . . organization!!! Sorry to beat around the bush, but how you manage your time is how happy you will be with your grades.

The first step to organization is having a clean, organized desk. (The college is generous enough to supply this in its raw form; it's up to you to organize it.) Also, make sure you're away from distractions when you study. You'll hear kids complain that they had to study four hours straight. This work could have been done in two hours if they hadn't been studying in a social place. Put all your notes for each class in one place, and keep a calendar with study times blocked out.

There are a few aspects of studying at college that are extremely different from high school studying. Unlike high school, you've got to capture class time. If you miss even one day of class, it'll take you days to catch up.

The professors give you a syllabus that outlines your homework for the whole semester. If you goof off for even a day or two, you'll understand why we call the syllabus "The Little Engine That Could"; that baby never stops coming at you, and it'll run you over if you look away long enough.

By the way, don't let the "weekend" fool you. Just because it's Saturday doesn't mean the work turns off. If you want your weekend free, you've gotta work for it.

The biggest difference is probably how you study. You can't just memorize stuff; you've got to understand it fully. I found this out real quick when my anatomy professor told the class that our exam was a four- to five-page essay on "the effects of hemoglobin on the left ventricle." If you don't know it, you're dead.

Well, I've got to move on because Time Consumer awaits. But let me say this: All the stuff I've told you isn't as intimidating as it sounds. If you are consistent and organized, there's always time for other activities. And, once you get into the swing of things, the good grades will come.

I'll catch you later.

Your bro,
Albert Einstein

A Word about Studying

It's the most dangerous bus on campus—it has run over more students than any other bus. Greyhound? School bus? No—it's the bus you will board the first day of every class . . . the SYLLABUS.

Make friends with your syllabus. It's your professor's day-by-day description of what you'll be expected to read, write, and report on that semester. Those who do what the syllabus says ride that bus to college success. Those who don't get run over by it.

The big difference between high school and college is that you are expected to manage your own academic life. No teacher nagging you to do it, no heavy-breathing parent standing over you. Your map is that syllabus. Plan your life and your time by it.

If you manage your study life well, you'll win yourself a lot more freedom to do things you want to do. Here are some simple "how's":

1. Learn it in class. Most people attend the class and plan to learn it later. Why waste that time? Listen 100 percent . . . concentrate . . . ask about what you don't understand.
2. Take excellent notes, underscoring what the prof emphasizes.
3. Review new material the same day. Try to make it yours right after you have heard the lecture on it.
4. Do the worst first. It's great for morale to get the most dreaded job out of the way.

The Bible sums up the secret of championship studying: "Whatever you do [being in class, taking notes, reviewing], work at it with all your heart, as working for the Lord, not for men [the professor or your parents]" (Col. 3:23).

So does this 100 percent approach make you a slave to your studies? No! It makes you the boss . . . and it makes you free!

True Friends

Dear Brad,

Whew! I just had the greatest time with my friends. We got some Chicago-style stuffed pizza, went Christmas shopping, played a little ice-football, and ran around the campus singing "Auld Lang Syne" at the top of our lungs until Public Safety gave us a citation for noise pollution.

How are the friends back home? I heard Jamie just got his driver's license. I'm never driving in town again. Just kidding! How's everyone handling the countdown to graduation? Are the seniors still coming to school?

Well, Brad, I'm writing you this time to report yet another observance I have soaked in here at college—the difference between friendships in high school and friendships in college.

When you're in high school, if you want to get together with a friend, you call him or her and set up a time when you can hang out. It's a little different here; you live with your friends! Now before you get too excited about this idea, let me remind you of something. You live with your family. So, to understand what friendship is like when you are living with your friends, compare it to what it's like living with your family.

This is a scary thought if you think about it too much, isn't it? In high school, you usually see your friends after you have taken your shower, used your deodorant, and brushed your teeth. You see each other while you're at your best. When you live with your family, they see you at all your moments. They have to take the good with the bad. This is the way it is when you are living with your friends in college. They're going to know that you use fourteen acne pads each night. They're going to know about your pink Miss Piggy toothbrush. They're going to know about those little fat deposits you hide so well. Perhaps these thoughts are a little frightening, but there is a bright side.

Think about your best friend in high school. Why is he or she your best friend? Probably because you know almost everything about each other and you still love each other's company. If this is the case, think of how many "best friends" you'll have in college. Trust me . . . you'll know who your true friends are because they will still want to hang out with you even after they find out about Miss Piggy. In short, true, close friendship comes from accepting each other's faults because you know you have just as many.

The last thing I'll tell you is to be careful about who you hang out with. A very wise man once said (I think it was Dad), "Tell me your friends, and I'll tell you your future."

Your bro,
The Doug Man

A Word about True Friends

When I'm at the airport to fly to Chicago, I find that there are a lot of nice planes there. Some are bigger than the one I'm ticketed for; others are newer or leaving sooner. But that doesn't matter. I need to pick the one that's going where I want to end up.

It's that way with college friends. Unlike high school friends, college friends tend to be yours for life. And even if you never see them again, their influence will mark you for life. Because you're away from home, your college friends virtually become your family.

So choose them well. Make sure they're going where you want to end up—in your values, your character, your relationship with God.

And don't ruin the beauty of friendship by letting your friends take over your life. If you do, you'll soon be so far behind that you'll be left with two lousy choices: Forget your friends to survive academically, or die academically—in which case you won't even be where your friends are!

A lot of people love to sing that lyric, "Friends are friends forever when the Lord's the Lord of them." In college, you can do more than sing the song—you can live it!

Mixing Oil and Water

Dear Brad,

Do me a favor tonight. Go into the kitchen, get a cup of oil and a cup of water, then mix them together. When you're finished with this, go ask the school bully if he'll go hang out with the ballet class. And when you're done with that, go ask the London Philharmonic if they'll consider asking Eddie Van Halen to be their new conductor. Once you've tried all of these scenarios (if you're that gullible), you may start to get the picture about how similar my roommate and I are.

Let's see, where can I start? I like rock and roll; he likes classical. I hang up pictures of Bo Jackson; his posters are "Countries of the World." Our temperaments couldn't be more different: I'm outgoing; he's quiet. To be honest, you probably couldn't find two people as different as we are. You know what, though? So far we've gotten along like brothers instead of enemies. How can two people so different get along so well? Well, we both learned some things in the early going.

First of all, we both realized we could learn things from one another. He never knew he could be so interested in the chord progression to "Louie, Louie." And I never knew I could be so interested in learning how to iron.

Here's a big reason we're getting along: patience. For instance, as far as the dorm room goes, I like the, ahem, "lived in" look. He prefers the hospital waiting room approach. So what did we decide on? Cockroaches or cleanliness? Well, our views on the room aren't that extreme, but they are different. But because we are patient and have reached a compromise with one another, we've reached a medium somewhere between sanitized and 1946 Nagasaki.

I've saved the biggest factor for getting along with your roommate until last: You've got to respect each other. I assume he doesn't want me wearing his underwear. He assumes I don't like him eating spaghetti in my bed. By being respectful of and courteous to each other, we hardly ever fight.

Notice the words "hardly ever." Yes, though things are usually smooth, you can expect at least one mammoth argument per semester. But fear not . . . things usually blow over soon enough as long as you're fair and understanding with each other.

Before I leave you, dear brother, I'll give one last, vital instruction: pray about your roommate. This is the most powerful and effective thing you can do before you meet the person you'll spend the whole school year with.

Your ex-roommate,

A Word about College Roommates

The Matchmaker has your name. Soon you'll see who you got matched up with.

The Matchmaker is your heavenly Father. The match is your roommate—if you've been praying for God to pick him. "The steps of a good man are ordered by the Lord" (Ps. 37:23, KJV), that must include a step as important as who you'll live with every day.

Pray so you can walk into that room on Day One with anticipation rather than anxiety. "Let's see what person God thought I needed to spend the next year with."

Don't be surprised if it's someone very different from you. "As iron sharpens iron, so one man sharpens another" (Prov. 27:17). God knows how much you can grow by adapting to another person's needs, tastes, idiosyncrasies, and priorities. You might say, "I already had to do that with my brother." Ah yes, but at college there's no parent to arbitrate the negotiations!

If you hit some frustrations in your relationship, don't let the frustrations build up. Confront them while they're small.

Learning to love and live with a roommate is one of the best growing opportunities you have had in your life so far. By praying for your roommate—even before you know who it is—you allow God to do the choosing. By praying with your roommate through all kinds of challenges, you can tear down walls and build lifetime bonds.

I got to thinking how awesome it would be to have Jesus for a roommate. Here's what He would be like:

> In humility consider others better than yourselves. Each of you should look not only to your own interests, but also to the interests of others. Your attitude should be the same as that of Christ Jesus. (Phil. 2:3-5)

If Jesus lives in you, then the person you'll live with could have a roommate like that. Let Jesus move into that dorm when you do . . . through you.

Christian College
Peer Pressure

Dear Brad,

How's life treating my favorite senior? Is the academic pressure getting to be too much for you? (Yeah, right.) Is the dog still alive?

It's always encouraging to me when I'm reminded how you've stood up against the peer pressure that's so strong in high school. Thank God I made it through high school without too many bruises myself. I'm glad you've known what it's like to stand up to peer pressure, because it doesn't go away once you get to college . . . even a Christian college.

There are some pressures you'll feel from those around you that are unique to Christian schools. They aren't the same pressures you've had to deal with in high school, but they are pressures that can cause you to sin.

One big question asked at a Christian college is, What kind of a Christian will you be? It's an important question, and there's pressure to be at both extremes.

Some will ridicule you because you try too hard to serve Jesus. They will encourage you to "take it easy" and "enjoy the ride." If you don't, they'll rail on you. Does this sound familiar? Jesus' disciples were constantly persecuted because they were so fervent about their commitment to Christ. Most of the time these people will be making fun of you for the simple reason that they know you've given everything up for Jesus . . . and they haven't.

You'll feel pressure from the "super Christians" to be perfect. Are you in the right Bible study? Are you in enough ministries? Are your devotions long enough? These people are more concerned with how you look on the outside than how you look on the inside.

These "super Christians" will introduce you to one of the greatest pressures of all at a Christian college—getting into useless arguments. These "Christian cat fights" are ridiculous. Each person will recklessly cling to some theological view and then beat it to death over a matter of hours. Think of how many better things could be done with your time!

Though I've only hit on pressures that are unique to Christian colleges, this does not mean the usual human pressures disappear. Sexual pressure is as strong as ever. Pressure to compromise any belief is a constant force. These don't go away; you'll deal with them your whole life.

So what to do? How do you avoid these extremes? Find a medium. Know that it's your responsibility to constantly challenge yourself and grow in the Lord. Then know that there's no way you can be the "perfect Christian." Know Jesus' first command is to love Him.

Next time I write I'll try to cover peer pressure at a secular college. Until then, hang in there and stick to your guns.

Your bro,

A Word about Christian College Peer Pressure

Squeeze an egg as hard as you can—and have a lot of fun cleaning the yolk off the walls, the floor, and you. Now . . . take a hard-boiled egg and squeeze it as hard as you can. No cleanup, no splat. Two eggs, both squeezed—what's the difference? One is "squeeze-proof" because it is solid at the center.

It's important that you enter college solid at the center . . . solid because you've settled your personal convictions and won't change them. The surprise is that there is so much moral and spiritual "squeeze" at a Christian college.

On one side, you'll feel pressure from students who are "playing world," abusing their new freedom to sample sin. They really can't handle their first opportunity to make choices outside their hometown cocoon. They are trying so hard to prove they are free that they become slaves to freedom, always having to choose the opposite of Christian choices. These "slaves to freedom" will be pressuring you to "loosen up." If you're solid at the center, you'll stick to Galatians 5:13: "Do not use your freedom to indulge the sinful nature."

On the other side, you'll be squeezed by people who think there is only one narrow way to be spiritual. They're slaves, too . . . slaves to formulas, externals. God's plan for His body is variety (1 Cor. 12), yet these people will insist that everyone pray, worship, serve, and believe exactly alike. Sometimes they will "play Holy Spirit," trying to help Him convict everyone of sin. Later on, folks like these divide churches over minor issues. "It is for freedom that Christ has set us free. Stand firm, then, and do not let yourselves be burdened again by a yoke of slavery" (Gal. 5:1).

There's a simple bottom line question you'll have to settle on this side of moving day: Who are you going to please? If you decide once and for all that the answer is Jesus—only Jesus—you'll never collapse . . . no matter how hard you're squeezed.

Secular College Peer Pressure

Dear Brad,

It is I! Yes, it's time for another letter from Doug. I sure hope you're reading these.

Last time I wrote I tried to clue you in on some pressures you might face when you get to college. So what about your friends that are going to a secular college? I probably don't have to tell you there will be as much, if not more, pressure there.

Though many secular pressures rear their head at a Christian college, these pressures seem much more intense at a secular institution.

First of all, there will be the obvious pressure against Christianity itself. The secular world does not like Jesus, and that fact won't be different at a secular school. Most teachers, clubs, and other students will not support an outward show of Christianity. This would make it pretty easy to sink into Christian oblivion.

Because there will be so little support of a Christian lifestyle, it will be easy to stop having devotions and going to church. When no one else is doing these things, it makes a good rationalization to stop doing them yourself.

There are the obvious pressures like drinking and sex. These could be the trickiest pressures of all. You can go to your secular college with strict sexual standards, but soon you will find out that many, including your roommate, won't think twice about having sex on a regular basis. This fact could make a nice rationalization to let up on your own standards and justify this by telling yourself, "at least I'm not having sex."

How do you deal with these pressures? It sounds simple but is very hard—you've got to stick to your guns. Go to college knowing what is right and wrong, and stick to that. The moment you start comparing yourself to other people instead of Jesus is the moment you'll start to fall.

Well, I hope this letter helps if any of your friends have any questions. See ya later.

Your bro,

[signature: Doug]

A Word about Secular College Peer Pressure

If you tried to play football or soccer on a field with no boundaries, you wouldn't have a game.

Most people at secular colleges are playing life as if there were no boundaries. The result is chaos. Because you belong to Jesus Christ, you need to know where your boundaries are. There won't be any around you, so you'll have to bring them inside you.

When you're God's ambassador to a secular school, you need the "Conqueror's Survival Kit." It has five tools in it:

1. *A Firsthand Faith. Your parents' or your church's faith won't survive the pressure. Be sure you have an*

active, growing, personal relationship with Jesus. If your faith depends on your environment, "Goodbye, Jesus."

2. A Consistent Stand. The best way to reduce peer pressure is to take the same stand every time. Once people see there is only one you, they will usually lay off and let you be that person.

3. A "No Compromise" Morality. Satan usually destroys a Christian by erosion, not explosion. He will try to wear you down to sins you never thought you would commit just by getting you to make a series of little compromises. Say no to the first compromise; it's the easiest one to resist.

4. A Support Team. Peer pressure is your friend if the group is going God's way. Go wherever you have to go to find a group of young believers who share your convictions.

5. A "Make a Difference" Attitude. God sends you to a college to change your environment, not just to survive. If your goal is just to survive, you won't. When you're actively fighting for people's lives, you know compromise is too costly.

There's a challenging Christian song that asks, "Will you be the one to stand when those around you fall? Will you be the one to take His light into a darkened world?" Say to Him today, "I will be the one!"

Mom and Dad

Dear Brad,

They are the saints who changed our diapers and taught us how to walk. The kindred spirits who endured the monster we call a five-year-old. The loving hand that guided us through (yuk) junior high. The firm yet affirming voice we heard through our adventures in high school. The nurturing love that has been with us since birth. Yes, Brad, it is that time. Today I'm going to write to you about those wonderful creatures we call parents.

Whether or not we have always agreed with the way they have reared and disciplined us, we owe them a lot. At the bare minimum, they provided us with food, shelter, and security for eighteen years. So, we love them and they love us.

No matter what kind of relationship you have with Mom and Dad, it's going to change once you get to college. Things don't necessarily get better or worse, they just change. I'm writing today to prepare you (hopefully) for how things will change with you, how they'll change for Mom and Dad, and how you can keep the relationship working.

The big change for you will be not having Mom and Dad around. Though you may not think so now, a spell of the ol' homesickness might set in. This homesickness is not anything to feel stupid about; almost everyone feels it whether they admit it or not. You just can't let these feelings convince you you're in the wrong place. Most of all, you shouldn't let the anticipation of these feelings be a factor in what school you go to. Once you're at college, the feelings gradually subside. Trust me.

Though we are affected by Mom and Dad's absence, I am sure they are affected even more by ours. Parents go through what I call the "Sunrise, Sunset" syndrome. All of a sudden their baby has grown up and is about to leave the nest, and this is hard for them (although Mom and Dad seemed strangely exuberant in my case!). It's your responsibility to keep this in mind as you head to college.

One way to be sensitive to this is to keep them up to date about what's happening in your college life. This means more to them than you think. By filling them in once in a while, you put them more at ease and find that they trust you more because of your honesty.

So what's the best way to have a good relationship between you and the folks while you're at college? Leave a good relationship at home. It makes things a lot easier.

You can also basically ensure a healthy relationship if you do one important thing before you leave: Don't set foot out the door until you guys have agreed on what your goals are for college. Decide what you're going for and what they're expecting you to get from it. You'll find clearing these things up beforehand prevents a lot of grief.

Well, it's time for me to get going—I promised Mom and Dad I'd call them tonight.

Your bro,

A Word about Mom and Dad

Amputation is painful . . . especially if it's your son or daughter who's being cut off.

Mom and Dad have sort of gotten used to having you around for eighteen years. Then one day you and your stuff are gone. You go to a New World full of new people and experiences. Your parents stay in the Old World, missing being a part of your days.

It's an adjustment. But it doesn't have to be an amputation . . . if you don't let your new busyness cut you off from Mom and Dad. So . . .

- Don't become a stranger. Keep them up-to-date on your rapidly changing life. If you don't, they will have a hard time understanding you at a time when you really need them. Besides, you need their outside perspective. "Keep your father's commands and do not forsake your mother's teaching. Bind them upon your heart forever" (Prov. 6:20-21).
- Don't just use them as your personal rescue squad. Your parents' number is not 911. It's not much of a relationship if you only call when you're choking financially, expecting them to jump out of the ambulance with a checkbook and administer financial CPR.
- Don't fill up your breaks with everybody else. They count the days until you're home. Save a little time for them.
- Don't expect them to cancel the Family Constitution for you. When you come home, you're going to

have to adjust to some expectations and restrictions you don't have at college. Your parents need to adjust to your new independence, too. When there's conflict between your freedom and their expectations, talk it out . . . agree on some compromises.

God's command to honor your father and mother is for life. When you get married or financially independent, obey is not the issue anymore. But honor is always there.

So don't let your evacuation be an amputation. Treat Mom and Dad with respect, and you may graduate again . . . from just being their kid to actually being their friend.

Studying Your Professors

Dear Brad,

Ooh boy, it's getting cold here. It's so cold that I'm doing that thing you thought I'd never do. That's right—I've abandoned all style, all coolness. I've taken that step into silliness. It's horrible, yes . . . but it had to be done. I'm sorry Brad, but there's nothing you can do to stop me; I have already committed the unspeakable horror of horrors!

Yep, I'm wearing my earmuffs. Laugh if you must, but prepare yourself for the day when you will meet your furry foe.

Well, enough silliness. Today I'm writing you to discuss perhaps the most beneficial thing I've learned in my stay at college: studying my professors.

I know that sounds a little backward. You're supposed to study your books, right? This is true, but I think you'll find getting the grade you desire a little easier if you study your professors.

Let me explain.

College freshmen get the impression that their professors are these well-oiled machines who only spout facts, grade papers, and live under their classroom desk. But believe it or not, professors are people! That's right, they've got flesh, bones, and even feelings. If you take this fact into account, you've taken your first step in studying your professors.

So what exactly do I mean, "study your professors"? It's as simple as this: Spend the first week of classes figuring out just what your profs want and expect of you. Ask questions to find out what aspects of each course are important to them, and keep those aspects in mind when test time rolls around.

When talking to your professors, I think you'll find just how human they are. Though you need to treat them with a certain amount of professional respect, they appreciate it when you talk to them as a friend. And who knows? You may end up with a friend . . . for life.

Keep studying and hang in there.

Your bro,

A Word about Professors

It's 8:00 A.M. on a Monday morning in August—your first class in college. In your hand is a new, untested Bic pen . . . on your desk is an untouched notebook and a twenty-five pound textbook . . . and in front of you is the Giver of Grades, the Keeper of the Academic Keys—your professor.

Prepare to get to know this person. Knowing your subject will not be enough . . . you will need to know what this professor expects, emphasizes, and examines. Some profs you will take to, others will turn you off. But don't let that change your commitment to know your professor. "Professorology" involves:

1. *Displaying interest in the subject.* You may not care much about his or her subject, but your professor

probably cares a lot about it. Whether or not the subject lights your fire, take good notes, ask good questions, make good comments.
2. Asking for help. When you're struggling, ask for help . . . immediately.
3. Showing respect. "Submit yourselves for the Lord's sake to every authority" (1 Pet. 2:13). Be friendly, say thank you, and ask about the things that seem to be important to your professor.

Every once in a while, you may find a professor you just can't handle. Remember those helpful letters TTSP—"This Too Shall Pass."

"Good morning, class."

Oops—your first class has begun.

"This is Psychology 101."

Well, yeah . . . but you know it's more than that. It's Professorology 101!

Living within Your Means

Dear Brad,

Hey, uh, Brad? Could you do me a favor? I'm kinda running low on cash, and I thought you could hit up Mom and Dad for me. I can't do it because I've, well . . . let's just say I'm overdrawn.

Budgeting money is something important to learn before you get to college. Take it from someone who's still learning. This letter is to help give you a clue on how to budget money . . . before you get here.

The first thing you've got to do, of course, is see how much money you have to work with. If you have enough to cover your fixed expenses, good for you. If you don't, you may want to get a part-time job. Don't get one just for spending money; you'll never have time to spend it.

Once you know how much you have to work with, write down all of the things you'll be spending money on during the semester. It works best if you make categories like fun, food, books, car (if you have one), toiletries, dates, etc. Write down how much you will spend in each category, and stick to that amount. Trust me: The time you stop writing down your expenses is the time you'll run out of money.

A big benefit that comes from budgeting your money is your parents' trust. If, when you beg them for money, you can show them where it all went, they may be more compassionate about your situation.

Well, I've got to run—I've got to go make out a budget so I can ask Mom and Dad for more money.

Your bro,

Doug

A Word about Living within Your Means

Budget is not a four-letter word. In fact, it's a friendly word. It builds your parents' trust, gives you a financial map to keep you from getting lost, and prevents panic later on. Manage your money well, and you will have the most convincing proof of all that you are an adult.

Money maturity begins by having a clear understanding with your parents of who is paying for what. That can head off some ugly budget wars.

Now that you are managing your finances, learn to think economy. "How can I make this amount of money go the farthest?" Discover the lower prices of store brands . . . make it to the school meals you've already paid for instead of buying outside frequently . . . buy snacks in quantity at the store instead of buying them from machines . . . look for cheap, creative date ideas . . . learn to clean and repair things instead of discarding them.

And don't forget God. The biblical starting point for giving to your Lord is 10 percent. If you give to the Lord's work right off the top, you'll find that the 90 percent will go miraculously farther than 100 percent that forgets God.

You say, "But money is so tight at college—I can't afford to give to God." You can't afford not to! "Bring the whole tithe into the storehouse. . . . Test me in this . . . and see if I will not throw open the floodgates of heaven and pour out so much blessing that you will not have room enough for it" (Mal. 3:10).

Ron

Going Steady

Dear Brad,

"Brad and Fredericka, sitting in a tree, k-i-s-s-i-n-g, first comes love, then comes marriage, then comes the baby in the baby carriage." These fine lines of classical literature bring back fond grade-school memories. You know, it's funny how harmless these words seem to a little guy in third grade and how terrifying these same words are to a big guy in thirteenth grade. I'll explain later.

There is no question in my mind that one of the things every precollege freshman worries about before he or she gets to school is what their love life is going to be like and how it will be different from what they experienced in high school. I know my future love life was a big worry of mine before I got to college. Come to think of it, it still is.

One thing you've got to remember is that college freshmen were high school seniors just three short months before they got to college. The antics you think you will be escaping once you leave high school are not going to miraculously disappear the moment you get on campus. In fact, it takes just about the whole freshman year before things significantly change. But fear not, they do.

Dating is an interesting thing in high school. A lot of the relationships are based on a "what have you done for me lately?" attitude. This may not be true in every case, but it seems as if before you ask someone to "go steady" with you, you need to know the person's car model, position on the sports team, and a brief family history. Though these attitudes do not automatically disappear once you get to college, they do subside quite a lot, and the ones who stick with these attitudes seem to be the ones who end up with the short end of the stick.

Let me explain.

There is a scary phenomenon that occurs in 91.2 percent of college women. It's called "aauuggghhifIdontgetahusbandsoonIwillendupasanoldmaid" syndrome. When you hear of a woman who has succumbed to this deadly disease, quarantine yourself from her. To be truthful, the same thing happens in guys, but they don't want to admit it.

People have a totally different dating agenda at college. Instead of thinking, How good will I look with this person? smart people start thinking, Would this be a person who would love and respect me for the rest of my life? Would this be a person I would like to have my children look up to? Eventually, these questions become more important than having a Chippendale's physique.

Don't get me wrong. There will always need to be some physical attraction between people; it's just not as important as it used to be. So, all of a sudden, you may see "Johnny the Geek" with the homecoming queen. Don't laugh, I've seen it happen. I call it "the revenge of the average looking."

I know, I know. Marriage seems so far away. You're still heading toward graduation! Why do you need to be worried about marriage now? You don't yet, but before you know it that huge gap you think there is between how you feel now and how you'll feel when you're ready to be married closes up. Scary, but true.

Well, I've gotta get going. But before I do, I'm going to tell you the best advice I ever heard about dating at college: "Never steadily date someone you wouldn't consider committing the rest of your life to."

It's a tall order, but in the long run it may save you a lot of grief . . . and maybe even lead you to the person God has chosen for you.

Your bro,
Doogie

A Word about Going Steady

According to ancient Indian tradition, when you die you go to the Happy Hunting Ground. Arriving on your college campus, you may think you've reached the Happy Hunting Ground without dying . . . at least if it's the opposite sex you're hunting.

But put your bow and arrow down. You'll miss a lot of relationships if you get swept into the Great Date Chase. Superficiality was for high school. College is your chance for real-lationships. The key is to focus on building friendships with the opposite sex, not romances. You make friends . . . let God make one of them into a romance.

When friendship is your agenda, a relationship can develop without the cat-and-mouse tension of romantic pursuit. Unlike date-chasing, friend-building . . .

- Focuses on making the other person feel important instead of trying to impress her. You can relax and be yourself.
- Isn't charged with the pressure of a physical agenda—"How far are we going to go tonight?" With the sexual thing a non-issue, you can really get to know each other as people.
- Can involve a group instead of a couple. Again, you can relax and be yourself more easily if you aren't in the pressure situation of trying to carry the evening by yourself.
- Helps a guy build up the confidence he needs for a deeper relationship without risking romantic rejection.
- Keeps a woman from the loneliness that results from not being asked out. Since friend activities are not the big deal a date is, there will be a lot more socially active nights.
- Gives you a chance to become the kind of person you want to marry someday.

Graduation from high school can mean graduation from the frustration and immaturity of the Great Date Chase into the better idea of friendship-building.

And you won't lose on romance either. Instead, you'll open the door to falling in love with a lifetime best friend.

Long-Distance Romance

Dear Brad,

OK, do you remember "the talk" about the birds and the bees? Well, I'm about to give you "the talk" on college long-distance romances. I wish I was more of an expert on the subject, but maybe I've gone through enough so far to try to give you the lowdown. So do you want to hear what I've learned so far? . . . That's OK; keep reading anyway.

First, I'd like to tell you my feelings on those brave souls who leave a love at home in the hopes that a long-distance relationship will flourish. In the beginning of the year the guys on my floor had a meeting. We talked about a bunch of different stuff including bathroom etiquette, self-defense tactics for those times your roommate has had a bad day, and—you guessed it—relationships.

Our floor leader asked every freshman who had a girlfriend at home to raise his hand. Just about half of them waved their arms frantically. Then he asked how many of these guys had a strong relationship that could last through thick and thin. Again, about half of the guys raised their hands.

Two months later we had another floor meeting, and the first question asked was "OK, how many of you have girlfriends at home?" Out of the twenty guys who had raised their hands at the beginning of the year, only two raised them this time! What happened?

The answer to that question is a goldfish. That's right, a goldfish. Do you remember when the family went on vacation to California, and we saw those huge fish swimming in a pond? When we asked Mom what kind of fish they were, she told us they were goldfish. How could that be? The only goldfish we had ever seen were the little ones we brought home from the carnival and put in a bowl. After Mom explained that, no, these goldfish did not take steroids, she told us that the goldfish adapts its size to its surroundings. To put it simply, once the fish's world got bigger, he grew to his potential.

Though it may sound like a cliché and a "college thing to say," the fact is your world gets much bigger when you get to college. No matter how strong you believe your relationship at home is, there is almost always a "bigger fish." By not at least trying to open up your options, you are staying in that small goldfish bowl and may be cheating yourself out of the best relationship with a woman you could ever have.

Before I sign off so I can go meet my goldfish, I'll tell you my final advice: At least give yourself the option to date other people by the time you get to college. If your relationship back home is as strong as you think it is, it will stand the test of time and miles.

Your bro,
Romeo

A Word about Long-Distance Romance

Long-distance phone calls cost a lot. So do long-distance romances.

In fact, they usually cost someone a broken heart. Why do people go to college committed to someone back home? Obviously, it's because of some deep feelings—probably the closest feelings to real love they have ever felt.

But there's a painful miscalculation in going to the New World with a "Taken" sign on. You're underestimating how much and how fast you will change there. In only a few months, you will not be the same person who left for college. The girl you left will either change in that period of time or stay the same because she stayed in the Old World. In either case, a gap will develop. And it will hurt.

Locking yourself up in a steady relationship "back there" sets you up for all kinds of emotional struggle—guilt over other attractions, frustration over communication problems, confusion over mixed feelings, "schizo-ness" from trying to live in two different worlds.

Because your steady and the Old World is all you can see, you'll be reluctant to renegotiate an open relationship. But listen to the voices who have seen the New World, who know what's there. They will almost unanimously say, "Come with your options open." If what you have at home is real, it will stand the test. If God has someone else for you in the New World, you'll avoid breaking one—and maybe two—hearts.

Sexual Pressure

Dear Brad,

Well, it's getting toward the end of your senior year. . . . Have you gone crazy yet? Hang in there; it'll be done before you know it.

So far I've written enough letters for you to at least get a picture of what it's like to go to college. Some stuff has been serious, some not so serious. This letter, though, is one of the most important ones I will send.

A senior in high school is certainly no stranger to sexual pressure and, a lot of the time, is no stranger to sexual experiences. High school is a place where, all of a sudden, who slept with whom is an important topic. I don't know what you think college is going to be like, Brad, but I just thought I'd tip you off a little about what to expect.

Let's face it . . . we're sexual creatures. You are, I am, and, yes, even our parents are. I know you've heard this before, but it's real important that you accept this fact before you confront any kind of major sexual pressure. God made us like this, and he doesn't make mistakes. Once you know and accept this, it's easier to deal with the sexual pressures unique to college.

I guess the best way I can explain the difference between sexual pressure here and in high school is to talk about cookies. Remember when we were little and we wanted a cookie, but Mom wouldn't let us have one? We were afraid to go against what she said because to get a cookie we had to get it out of the cookie jar. This brought a certain amount of risk in getting a cookie. We'd stay away from the cookie jar because we were afraid we would get caught . . . not because we cared whether it was right or wrong.

Once you get to college, there's no one watching the cookie jar anymore. Within obvious limits, you can take a lot of cookies—almost whenever you want—without anyone slapping your hand. There's no one watching you anymore; almost every decision you will make will be credited to what you believe.

This sexual responsibility is a personal one. Like every other God-given responsibility, you and you alone will be held accountable for how you use it. But how can you avoid giving in to this huge rush of new sexual pressure?

Know what you believe and why you believe it before you ever set foot on campus. If you resist sexual immorality for the single reason that God says it's wrong and because God wants sex to be kept for marriage, you're at much less of a sexual risk. If you're avoiding it for any other reason, you'll be in trouble.

As in any other decision, it's extremely important to be honest with yourself. Decide now what your feelings about sexual morals are, and adjust them where they need adjusting.

I've got to hit the road, but I want to ask you to keep the cookies in the cookie jar for now. They taste a lot better after dinner.

Your bro,

God hasn't changed His mind about sex.

"Marriage should be honored by all, and the marriage bed kept pure" (Heb. 13:4). "It is God's will that you should . . . avoid sexual immorality" (1 Thess. 4:3).

The Inventor of sex has put a fence around it called marriage. Society wants to tear down the fence . . . your hormones encourage you to tear down the fence . . . and your freedom and friends at college will increase the pressure to forget the fence and "do it." If you do, you will give up the specialness of sex—and it's the specialness that makes it great.

My son has a baseball card collection. His most valuable cards are those that are either rare or in mint condition. By choosing the oftentimes unpopular road of purity, you're rare. As more and more people around you become more and more sexually active, you'll be tempted to feel that rare is weird. It's not. Rare is valuable. Keep yourself valuable and in "mint condition" for your future wife.

Remember that you are on the threshold of a new beginning. Whatever you may have done morally in high school can be put behind you now. That's what Jesus died on the cross for—to forgive our sins and to start us over with a clean slate. God says, "The blood of Jesus, his Son, purifies us from all sin" (1 John 1:7). If you turn from any past wrongs and give yourself to Christ, you can enter college's New World a new person.

With a new beginning, you need to put some guards around the "fence." You can keep sex special if:

1. You avoid the opportunity to mess up sexually. You cannot fight sin and flirt with it at the same time. So avoid prolonged times alone with a girl . . . don't allow yourself to get to a point where you're thinking beyond the boundaries of purity . . . let your standard be known right up front to anyone you spend a lot of time with.
2. You and God draw a physical line that you will not cross. Don't wait for your first college date or some passionate emergency. You and God (He lives in your body) settle the boundary now, before the pressure hits.
3. You watch what you watch and listen to. "Guard your heart, for it is the wellspring of life" (Prov. 4:23). If you are going to save sex for marriage, don't watch or listen to input that portrays the opposite.

On Day One of college, you're starting new. Start clean, with your heart set on purity. Crown Christ Lord of your love life and your glands every day. Then you will be able to go to sleep every night—including your wedding night—with no regrets.

Staying in Touch with God

Dear Brad,

I've got to write this letter quickly; I don't have much time for chit-chat. You wouldn't believe all the stuff I've got to do today. First, I've got to get to history on time. Then, I'll scarf down my lunch and head to my literature class just in time to get a seat before class starts. Then it's on to physics (hooray!) to get my daily dose of quantum theory. After class, I'll swiftly make my way to dinner and hopefully miss the line. And then, you would think, finally . . . the day is over. Not so fast. I've got a test to study for, a girlfriend to meet, and a workout that's calling my name. Then, finally, my day is over . . . the only problem being that it's 12:30 in the morning, and I've got to get up at 7:00 tomorrow.

With all this stuff to do, who's got time for anything else? This is why I'm writing to you, Brad, to remind you of what should be the most important, unpush-outable (is that a word?) activity of your day . . . your time with God.

I've got to be honest with you, Brad. These bits of advice I'm about to lay on you are not coming from a man who has stuck close to them. There are a number of times I have blown off my time with God, but I have been faithful enough to know it's important; hopefully I'll convince you it is too.

I guess the best way to avoid not spending daily time with God is to understand just how important it is in the first place. What if you didn't spend a consistent amount of time with your friends? The result would probably be a lack of closeness and an "out of touch" feeling. The same thing will happen in your relationship with God if you don't spend consistent time with him.

My time with God is a lot like my time with my history book. (What?) If I don't spend daily time with my history book, I fall behind, and it may result in my failing a test. The same applies to my devotions.

So with all I have to do during the day, how do I make sure my time with God doesn't go by the wayside? I follow a couple of easy steps.

First of all, I don't fool myself and say I'll do my devotions before I go to bed. I've tried this before. Half the time I would fall asleep, and the times I managed to stay awake I was so tired I didn't get anything at all out of reading my Bible. So, instead, I decided to do my devotions in the morning when I'm most alert. Not only could I stay awake better, but I could apply the words God spoke to me to the day I was about to face. So figure out when your best time is and give it to a few minutes of private Bible reading, prayer, and worship. God deserves it; after all, He gave His best to us.

I also make sure that this time with God is my priority for the day. Everything else can be pushed out . . . but not God.

What's made it fairly easy to stick by my time with God is this: Every day I ponder how my life would be if God decided to push me out. Scary thought.

Well, Brad, I've got to get going, but before I do I'll tell you the number one, absolutest, most positively best reason I spend time with my Lord every day—to learn to love Him.

Your bro,

They called it "The Rotor." It was a popular ride at the amusement park I loved to go to as a kid. "The Rotor" was like a giant washing machine tub. It was round and it rotated, faster and faster. Once it started spinning, the floor underneath you dropped away—the screams must have broken every window in the neighborhood. People were left suspended on a tiny ledge, flattened against the wall by centrifugal force.

Centrifugal force is what can destroy your closeness with God in college. Your life will be spinning faster there than it ever has before. Without you even knowing it, Jesus can be spun right to the outer edge of your life. And you will find yourself far from your Lord just when you need Him more than ever.

It doesn't have to be that way. Set a time each day that is Jesus' time and that no one else can have. Period. You may need to make your Jesus-time different for different days of the week because of your class schedule . . . but when it's Tuesday, put a "reserved for Jesus" sign on your regular Tuesday Jesus-time. Whenever possible, start your day with the Lord—He's a lot less likely to get squeezed out than later in the day, and you're a lot more likely to handle your day victoriously.

When your life is books, the Bible can become just another book. It's not. The Bible is God's love letter to you and your personal link to Jesus' love and leading. So when you pick up your Bible, picture Jesus in your room with you, speaking to you the words you're reading. And listen for an application you can make that day—a specific obedience, spawned by something He said.

Jesus teaches us to "seek first His kingdom and His righteousness, and all these things will be given to you as well" (Matt. 6:33). He will have a lot of competition for "first" when the college rotor starts speeding up. Don't let anyone or anything else have His time. No one else loved you enough to die for you.

It All Comes Down to This

Dear Brad,

I just can't believe it. The school year is coming to an end just as quickly as it started. It's hard for me to fathom that I'm one year closer to graduation and you're headed for your first year. I'm about to head into finals (death) week, so I think this will be the last letter for the year. Stop cheering, Brad.

Now that I think about it, I've written you about a lot of different things, haven't I? I pray some of them have helped in your precollege anxiety and that some will help in your mid-college anxiety. Though I covered a diversity of topics, I can tie all of these concerns together with two words: Trust Jesus.

I know that sounds simple and maybe even cliché, but out of all the advice I've written you this is the hardest thing to do. I see seniors here who have conquered all the ground I have mentioned, but have yet to trust Jesus.

I know they're easy to say, but what do the words trust Jesus mean? They mean you have given everything up to Him for His examination. Once you have done that, they mean you will do anything He asks you to, whether it means your major, your love life, or even how you will spend the rest of your life.

Jesus promises He will work everything out for the good for those who love Him, and He commands us to have total faith in Him. Though all this sounds great, I urge you not to give anything up until you mean it with all of your heart. But when you do, just watch how the One who loves you works.

I've gotta go, Brad; the books beckon. I love you, and I'll see you soon.

Your bro,

[signature: Doug]

A Word about What It Comes Down To

We've done our best to prepare you for the New World ahead. But no matter how much information you have, there's still a lot of "unknown" out there, right?

Well, that's OK, because now you have a wonderful chance to hang on to your Savior and see all that He can mean.

I remember driving into the mountains one night in a blinding blizzard. Hardly anyone was on the road . . . I wouldn't have been if I weren't speaking for a retreat in the mountains. The road was disappearing rapidly under heavy snow, and I could barely see beyond the hood of my car.

I got to my destination OK because of a snowplow. I got behind a big old snowplow and stayed close all the way. I couldn't see the road, but he could. And he was always just ahead of me, clearing the way.

That's what Jesus said He would do for you in one of His most excellent promises. I learned it in college, and I've claimed it over and over again when the road ahead was uncertain. Jesus said, "When He [the Good Shepherd] has brought out all His own, He goes on ahead of them" (John 10:4).

Everywhere you are about to go, Jesus your Shepherd will go there ahead of you to clear the way. He's already in your New World of college, getting your spot ready, your future friends ready, your needs cared for.

So everywhere you walk in your world of new beginnings, you will find your Shepherd's footprint.

That's all you need to know.

Postscript

Long before our daughter Lisa had her first day of college, she baked her first cake. Actually, she was only five years old when she announced to her mom and me, "I'm baking a cake for you —I'm doing it all by myself."

I could hear a lot of bustle and banging in the kitchen . . . then the aroma of something baking. I was reading in the living room when a sad-faced little girl entered, carrying her creation in front of her. "Here it is, Daddy," Lisa said with obvious disappointment.

I had been expecting a cake, but Lisa was delivering what looked like a giant cookie. My first thought—which I did not speak aloud—was, What happened? It did turn out to be a cake—but the flattest cake I'd ever seen.

And when Mom checked out the kitchen end of things, she found out why the cake never got past the bottom of the pan—Lisa had left out the baking powder. One missing ingredient made all the difference.

It could be the same in your life, especially as you face the new frontier of college. You could march into your future with most of the right ingredients—academic goals; positive attitude; things together with your family, your finances, and your friends—and life could still come out flat and you could go to bed a lot of nights feeling empty. You could be missing the one ingredient that makes all the difference.

Doug's letters from college have repeatedly referred to that Ingredient—actually, that Relationship. For every new beginning in his life there has been one Person who has gone with him: Jesus Christ.

Jesus is the one Ingredient you can't do without. You may head into your future without your parents, your high school friends, your room, your girlfriend, or your landmarks. But you need to go with Jesus in your heart.

The Bible refers to people who are "without hope and without God in the world" (Eph. 2:12). Actually, we're all without God unless we get rid of the wall between God and us. We've all felt that wall, but we're not sure why it's there.

It's like that husband and wife who were driving down the road, seated on opposite sides of the front seat. From the passenger side, the wife said, "Have you noticed that we don't sit close and cuddle like we used to?" To which her husband answered, "Well, I haven't moved."

God feels that way. He created us to live for Him, and we've lived for ourselves instead. In the words of the Bible, "Your iniquities have separated you from your God; your sins have hidden His face from you" (Isa. 59:2). We've moved away from God—He hasn't moved away from us. So we're lonely and no relationship seems to cure it because we're lonely for God. We're hurting because we're carrying pain He wants to share. We're empty because we have a hole in our soul only God can fill.

But there's this sin-wall—the accumulated distance of all the lies we ever told, the people we've ever hurt, the damaging words we ever spoke, the selfish things we ever said— all the sin of running our own lives.

Now, as you stand at the edge of your New World, is the time to get rid of the sin-wall between you and God, to be sure you enter every unknown with your hand in God's hand.

The same place in the Bible that described the "without God" problem doesn't stop there. It says, "But now in Christ Jesus you who once were far away have been brought near through the blood of Christ" (Eph. 2:13). When Jesus Christ died on that brutal cross, He was doing something about your God-wall—suffering the penalty for your sins, transferring all the guilt and hell of sin-living to Himself. The wall couldn't come down until the bill was paid, and Jesus paid it. You don't ever have to be far away from God again. You can be brought near.

Even though we moved away from God, He moved toward us. No one has ever loved you this much—He loved you so much "that He gave his one and only Son" so you may "have eternal life" (John 3:16). But like any love, it has to be responded to. One-way love won't work. John 3:16 says you have to believe in Him in order to get the forgiveness He paid for.

It's no accident that you have this book, or that you've read this far. God is reaching out to you right now. The most important question you could ask before you begin your future is, "How can I be sure I have this relationship with God?"

Let's get God's answer: "Repent, then, and turn to God, so that your sins may be wiped out [there goes the wall!], that times of refreshing may come from the Lord" (Acts 3:19). First, you have to turn away from running your own life. You have to tell God that you're ready to drop the junk. Then, with the junk gone, your hands will be free to grab Jesus and hold onto Him as your only hope—what it means to believe in Him.

You can open your life to God and His love right where you are. This isn't mere religion—it's Relationship, the Relationship you were made for. Jesus is yours for the inviting.

Not long ago I talked with a beautiful grandmother who is ninety-five years old. (Imagine your life plus seventy-five more years.) She's been through dozens of new beginnings, from leaving high school to rearing children to burying her husband to living in a wheelchair. But she has a glow and a smile that lights up a room.

I asked her what her favorite verse was in her well-worn Bible. She responded immediately, "Hebrews 13:8." Then, with a smile that made her look like a girl again, she quoted it—"Jesus Christ is the same yesterday and today and forever."

Her Jesus can be your Jesus. And He will be by your side through every change, every relationship, every crisis, and every need, and walk with you through life and, one day, into His presence. You'll need Him next year, and every year you live.

If Jesus has been the missing Person in your life, don't let Him be missing one more day. He's already moved in your direction—at the cross where he died for you. It's your move now.

If you would like to know more about knowing Christ personally as your Savior and Lord, write: Ron Hutchcraft Ministries, Inc., P.O. Box 1818, Wayne, NJ 07474-1818 (201-696-2161)